THE PRAYING BANK

THE PRAYING BANK

STEPHEN MORGAN

STEPHEN MORGAN PUBLISHING

The Praying Bank

Copyright © 2021 by Stephen Morgan

Unless otherwise noted, all Scripture references are from the King James Version of the Bible, copyright © 1979, 1980, 1982 by Thomas Nelson, Inc., Nashville, Tennessee.

PUBLISHER

Stephen Morgan Publishing

FIRST EDITION

ISBN-13: 978-1-7369632-0-3 - E-book

ISBN-13: 978-1-7369632-1-0 - Paperback

Printed in the United States of America

Publishing Consultants

Vike Springs Publishing Ltd.

www.vikesprings.com

For Bookings and Speaking Engagements, Contact Us:

Tel.: 001770-912-7877 Email: sankofalexis@gmail.com

The book is available at special discounts when purchased in bulk for promotions or as donations for educational and training purposes.

LIMIT OF LIABILITY/DISCLAIMER OF WARRANTY

DEDICATION

This book is dedicated to my son Josiah Praise Morgan, my Daughter Faith Annabelle Morgan, The Rockhill Church, Trinity International University of Ambassadors and all believers in our Lord Jesus Christ.

ACKNOWLEDGMENTS

First, I am extremely grateful to Almighty God for being my source of life, inspiration and success. To the great men and women of God who have functioned inordinately in my life, ministry and particularly for the support in putting together this volume: my family, Dr. & Mrs. Sonnie Badu, Dr. Jacqueline Mohair, Mrs. Wilhelmina Andoh, Christelle Tshishimbi, Prophet Samuel B. Addison, Lady Rev. Eunice B. Addison, Rev William B. Addison, Lady Rev. Sarah B. Addison, The Trinity International University of Ambassadors, The staff of Klasik Radio, and the members of The Rockhill Church: words cannot express my honest gratitude.

Thank you Mrs. Wilhelmina Andoh for writing the foreword of the book.

Thank you, Vike Springs for the professional editing, proofreading, formatting, interior designing, cover designing, publishing, printing and marketing.

Thank you Christelle Tshishimbi for the illustrations.

TABLE OF CONTENTS

FOREWORD

First, I would like to express my sincere gratitude to our Lord and Savior Jesus Christ for giving Pastor Stephen Morgan such grace and love for His people. Throughout the few years that I've known Pastor Morgan, I have discovered him to be a man of integrity and courage, who has genuine love for God and His people. Pastor Morgan's authentic love of Christ embellishes the aura of God's continuous presence around him. I can boldly affirm his faithfulness to serving God, his family, ministry and community.

I have personally observed Pastor Morgan develop deeply in the knowledge of God and demonstrate the valiant attributes of a genuine praying man. It is incredible; people who know or have encountered Pastor Morgan share amazing stories of his pure heart and service for Christ. Pastor Morgan possesses an exceptional anointing which is connected with the wisdom of God that succors him to comprehend the things in the realms of the spirit and tackle them with such boldness.

This humbling yet weighty book of prayer will enlighten and equip the body of Christ. Prayer indeed is a powerful tool, and irrespective of the challenges we encounter in life, this book will provide sturdy guidelines that allow you to be resilient in pulling down the demonic headlock on your life. This book postulates the much-needed prayer nuggets every Christian needs to overcome the various forms of spiritual attacks we encounter in life. This book is highly recommended for every home – a must-have!

Mrs. Wilhelmina Andoh
Mentor

INTRODUCTION

When a young man was growing up, his father opened a savings account for him which he could only access at the age of twenty-one. When he finally turned twenty-one, he went to the bank and withdrew all the money his father had saved for him, closed the account, and invested the money in a business venture. After six months of investing in the business, he became financially powerful. Unfortunately, he never sought to reopen his savings account and instead opted to keep the money safe at home.

After three years of running the business, he became a respectable young man in his community, until one day the unpredictable happened.

One Friday, after a hard day of work, he decided to go home early and treat himself to a relaxing afternoon. Around 9 pm his doorbell rang, which was very unusual, but upon looking at his security camera he realized it was his security guard. The door opened and five masked and armed men entered his house, one of them holding a gun to the head of the security guard.

They demanded all the money in the house and threatened to take the man's life if he didn't comply with their request within fifteen minutes. Finally, after series of beatings and torture he gave in. The armed men made off with the millions of dollars the young man had saved at home over the years. He said to himself, "If only I had put my money in the bank." But the unexpected had already taken place.

The above story can be related to today's Christianity. We pray using all our strength when things are either not working in our favor, or when we need a miracle from God. Once we receive what we need from God it's a goodbye to Him, forgetting the Bible's admonishing. [1 **Thessalonians 5:17** ("P*ray without ceasing*")]

> **"** *Prayer is never wasted but invested. Just as we save money in our physical or earthly bank, in the same vein we have to save up for prayer in our spiritual or heavenly bank. You might not see the results today but surely it will always speak for you someday.* **"**

The father of the young man in the above story invested ahead of time for the son but the son cut off the investment when he believed everything was going to work out for him.

Prayer is never wasted but invested. Just as we save money in our physical or earthly bank, in the same vein we have to save up for prayer in our spiritual or heavenly bank. You might not see the results today but surely it will always speak for you someday.

This book lays emphasis on investing in prayers and outlining ways of building up your prayer life as a believer.

WHAT IS PRAYER?

The question "What is prayer?" is connected to the communication between humanity (man) and divinity (a spirit being). Over time, a lot of different definitions have been given out for the above question.

The Century Dictionary defines prayer as "any spiritual communion ... including confession, petition, adoration, praise and thanksgiving." Prayer is also defined in Wikipedia as "an invocation or act that seeks to activate a rapport with an object of worship, typically a deity, through deliberate communication ('Prayer' n.d.)."[1]

From the above two definitions, we can clearly see that prayer is not only limited to Christians, because it is a communication that exists between a higher spirit being and man; therefore, Muslims, Theists, Hindus, Buddhists, and witch doctors all pray.

Dr. Sonnie Badu defines prayer as "developing a relationship with God and constantly communicating with Him."

From all of the above definitions, I would define prayer as a form of communication between humanity and divinity where once humanity speaks to divinity, humanity waits to hear from divinity before leaving His presence.

Prayer is not complete if a dialogue is not reached. Through our communication we end up building a relationship. The more you interact with another person or being, the stronger the bond you begin to build with each other. The communication has to be constant and consistent as any relationship that lacks communication breaks.

The more you develop a relationship with God the more you will get to know Him. Our constant and consistent interaction with God draws us closer to Him and improves our relationship with Him. He orders our steps and we walk with Him.

> "*My sheep hear my voice and I know them, and they follow me*"

> — JOHN 10:27

THE PRAYER MODEL

Most of the time, in our quest to receive answers to life's issues we communicate or share whatever we are battling with in hope of getting the answers that will equate to a lasting solution.

> *The strongest foundation a person can build when it comes to prayer is to have faith and believe in God*

The disciples, after walking with Jesus, approached Him and asked Him to teach them how to pray.

"Now it came to pass as He was praying in a certain place, when He ceased that one of His disciples said to

Him, 'Lord, teach us to pray, as John also taught his disciples.'"

— LUKE 11:1

The strongest foundation a person can build when it comes to prayer is to have faith and believe in God as indicated in the text below:

"But without faith it is impossible to please Him, for he who comes to God must believe that He is, and that He is a rewarder of those who diligently seek Him."

— HEBREWS 11:6

The life of Jesus on earth was very principled; He was never without prayer. He also commanded His day early in the morning with prayer and as such He was able to rule over His day with miracles and deliverances.

"Have you commanded the morning since your days began and caused the dawn to know its place. That it might take hold of the ends of the earth, and the wicked be shaken out of it?"

— JOB: 38:12-13

One of the disciples could not ask for anything more but for Jesus to teach them how to pray. Jesus did answer him with a prayer format known as the Lord's Prayer. In this chapter we are going to look at the model of prayer into detail.

In this manner therefore say: "*Our father in heaven, Hallowed be your name Your kingdom come, your will be done on earth as it is in heaven.*" (**Matthew 6:9-10**) In this verse Jesus urges us to put God first during prayer. We have to recognize God's existence in our life and His supremacy over us. We should recognize His reign in heaven and on earth and then activate God to occupy our heart, even though at times we end up driving God out. During this moment, we create an atmosphere for God's presence to dwell within us.

The Lord not only becomes the owner of our lives but also exists as our sole provider. He continuously gives us "our daily bread."

> **The heart of a human being is the dwelling place of God**

(**Matthew 6:11**) It only comes from God. In this verse Jesus is urging us to connect to the source of our livelihood. God has provided for man right from the time of creation until now. Before God created man, He created every provision that would support man's livelihood. Praying to God to give unto you your daily bread is just another way of recognizing Him as your Great Provider.

The heart of a human being is the dwelling place of God in our lives and as such, whenever we hold a grudge in our hearts we drive out the presence of God. So we must, "forgive us our debts, as we forgive our debtors." (**Matthew 6:12**) Our communication to Elohim through prayer is very important so that we always have the right standing with Him during prayer. Jesus draws our mind to the fact that before we ask God for forgiveness, we must first forgive those who have wronged us in any way. Whenever we come to the place of prayer we must LET GO AND LET GOD. According to John Hopkins researchers, un-forgiveness has its own health issues which include "heart attacks, blood pressure, depression and stress." [1]

> *"And do not lead us into temptation but deliver us from the evil one. For Yours is the kingdom and the power and the glory forever. Amen."*

> — MATTHEW 6:13 NKJV

"Test" is of God; "temptation" is of the devil. Jesus acknowledges this fact and encourages us to ask God during prayer to deliver us from evil. The deliverance of God always brings His power and glory into our lives.

It is important to note that when applying this format during prayer, we must come to a place of building a relationship with God. Once we build that relationship we begin to know, hear and understand Him when we communicate with Him. We become sensitive to His voice just as He recognizes our voice whenever we call.

The ability to pray is not automatic. We must learn how to pray unto God. Thankfully our Lord Jesus Christ has given unto us the kind of prayer that can touch heaven and make God's Kingdom come on earth for His will to be done on earth as it is in heaven. As I conclude this chapter, I want us to reflect on a prayer model written by one of the founding fathers of the United States of America, who also happens to be the 1st President: George Washington.

"O eternal and everlasting God, I presume to present myself this morning before thy Divine majesty, beseeching thee to accept of my humble and hearty thanks, that it hath pleased thy great goodness to keep and preserve me the night past from all the dangers, poor mortals are subject to, and has given me sweet and pleasant sleep, whereby I find my body refreshed and comforted for performing the

*duties of this day, in which I beseech thee to defend
me from all perils of body and soul.*

*Direct my thoughts, words and work. Wash away
my sins in the immaculate blood of the lamb, and
purge my heart by thy Holy Spirit, from the dross
of my natural corruption, that I may with more
freedom of mind and liberty of will serve thee,
the everlasting God, in righteousness and holiness
this day, and all the days of my life. Increase my
faith in the sweet promises of the Gospel. Give
me repentance from dead works. Pardon my
wanderings, and direct my thoughts unto thyself,
the God of my salvation.*

*Teach me how to live in thy fear, labor in thy
service, and ever to run in the ways of thy
commandments. Make me always watchful over
my heart, that neither the terrors of conscience,
the loathing of holy duties, the love of sin, nor an
unwillingness to depart this life, may cast me into
a spiritual slumber. But daily frame me more and
more into the likeness of thy son Jesus Christ, that
living in thy fear, and dying in thy favor, I may in
thy appointed time attain the resurrection of the
just unto eternal life. Bless my family, friends and
kindred unite us all in praising and glorifying thee
in all our works begun, continued, and ended, when*

we shall come to make our last account before thee
blessed Savior, who hath taught us thus."

Whether you are a president or a peon, that is a prayer to emulate, especially because it exemplifies the following ways to pray:

1.) PRAY HUMBLY

"I presume to present myself," the prayer begins. Jesus once told a story of a Pharisee and a tax collector who went to pray in the temple at the same time. The tax collector bowed his head and humbly begged for mercy while the Pharisee bragged to God that he was kind of a big deal—nothing like the tax collector.

Vs.9 Also, He spoke this parable to some who trusted in themselves that they were righteous, and despised others:

Vs.10 "Two men went up to the temple to pray, one a Pharisee and the other a tax collector.

Vs.11 The Pharisee stood and prayed thus with himself, 'God, I thank You that I am not like other men — extortioners, unjust, adulterers, or even as this tax collector.

Vs.12 I fast twice a week; I give tithes of all that I possess.'

Vs.13 And the tax collector, standing afar off, would not so much as raise his eyes to heaven, but beat his breast, saying, 'God, be merciful to me a sinner!'

Vs.14 I tell you, this man went down to his house justified rather than the other; for everyone who exalts himself will be [a]humbled, and he who humbles himself will be exalted.

— LUKE 18:9-14

Guess whose prayer impressed God most, according to Jesus?

2.) PRAY GRATEFULLY

Anytime you pray, even in the most desperate circumstances, you have multiple reasons to be grateful, even if it is only to pray simply for your life, breath, and to present your petitions to God. Similar to the prayer above, do not neglect any opportunity to give "humble and hearty thanks" for God's great goodness in keeping and preserving you through the previous night, and for giving you consciousness to perform the duties of the day and more.

3.) PRAY PENITENTLY

Many churches have excluded confession from public prayer and worship and that is, in my opinion, a great and grievous loss. As a result, many people neglect confession when they pray. Confessing our sins, like the prayer above, "Wash away my sins" and "purge my heart", is a helpful spiritual practice. It frees us, gives us a "do-over", and teaches us to walk in forgiveness and grace toward ourselves and others.

4.) PRAY SPECIFICALLY

When you communicate with God, your prayer must be specific. You must ask God to:

- Direct your thoughts, words and work.
- Increase your faith in the sweet promises of the Gospel.
- Provide you repentance from dead works. Pardon your wanderings and direct your thoughts unto Him.
- Teach you how to live in fear of Himself, to labor in His service, and to run in the ways of His commandments.
- Make you always watchful over your heart.
- Frame you into the likeness of His son Jesus Christ.

- Bless your family, friends and kin, and unite you all in praising and glorifying thee.

These are such helpful examples of thoughts, intentions and careful of expressions of prayer!

5.) PRAY HOPEFULLY

Prayer vibrates with hope and expectation of God's "great goodness," with the possibility of "righteousness and holiness," with "the sweet promises of the Gospel" and more[2]. Therefore, George Washington shows us that we must pray humbly, gratefully, penitently, specifically, and hopefully.

TYPES OF PRAYER

As we have dealt with the question of "What is prayer?", this chapter will deal with the various types of prayer we have and when a believer should activate each. Theologians categorize prayer into seven different types. They are:

1. Communion (all the time)
2. Supplication (humbly make your request known to God)
3. Intercession (intervening on behalf of others)
4. Spiritual Warfare — There are two types:
   - Dealing with yourself (Your Mind is the Battlefield & Repentance and Forgiveness)
   - Dealing with Satan and demons (Putting on the Full Armor & Binding & Loosening)
5. Prayers of Agreement (when you join your faith together in prayer)
6. Watch & Pray (continual state of awareness like a watchman on the wall)

7.   Prayers of Thanksgiving (showing your appreciation and gratefulness for all that the Lord has done for you)

In this chapter, I will be handling four types of prayer from the preaching series of Dr. Sonnie Badu of the Rockhill Church titled "**THE DYNAMICS OF PRAYER.**" [1] [2] [3]

This sermon outlines the four types of prayer mentioned earlier in this chapter:

1). COMMUNION

We must constantly pray to God. We have to keep engaging God on a daily basis in His highest tabernacle to look down on us. Be consistent and constant in communication with Him. Seek Him, find Him, and continuously call on Him. Your consistency develops a relationship with God; therefore giving Him access to you. "*That I may know Him and the power of His resurrection, and the fellowship of His sufferings, being conformed to His death*" (**Philippians 3:10**). Engage God on the altar and cease to engage man via social media.

2). **PRAYER BY MEDITATION**

Prayer by meditation was a type of prayer utilized by King David on a continuous basis. Meditation has more to do with the concept of intimacy. The Century Dictionary defines meditation as "close or continued thought; the turning or revolving of a subject in the mind; sustained reflection." When it comes to meditation you think about God's goodness, "I *will meditate on Your precepts, and contemplate Your ways.*" **(Psalm 119:15)** The more you meditate on the word of God, the more you begin to understand His ways.

3). **PRAYER BY CHANTING**

A lot of people have the perception that chanting is just for those who practice occultism. But Christians actually chant more than all other religions. Chanting is simply the repetition of words. As Christians, we chant during praise and worship through songs. The more you chant, the more God shows up, which is why you experience a manifestation. No matter what comes your way, please keep singing the prayer.

4). **SPIRITUAL WARFARE AND INTERCESSION**

Understand that since prayer is a form of communication between humanity and a deity, or a spirit, then when you are addressing the devil you do it through warfare prayers. You should not be gentle when it comes to addressing the devil. You should shout at the enemy because he has what belongs to you. He is trespassing, and causing confusion in your home. Some of the methods of warfare prayer are the clapping of hands and stamping of your foot.

> *You need to understand the dynamics of prayer or else you will miss the fire of God*

In conclusion, you need to understand the dynamics of prayer or else you will miss the fire of God. The revelation you have behind the prayer produces the results. Whenever we commune, meditate and chant during prayer we are offering it to God; however, when it comes to warfare, these prayers are directed to the devil and his agents.

4

PRAYER, THE BELIEVER'S LIFESTYLE

Knowing when to pray, where to pray and how we pray is paramount in the life of every believer. There are no restrictions when it comes to prayer. Paul urges us to pray without ceasing in I **Thessalonian 5:17**. The Greek word for "without ceasing" in I **Thessalonian 5:17** is '*adialeiptos*', which does not mean non-stop, but actually means **constantly recurring**. The moment we adapt to this concept it becomes a lifestyle.

Lifestyle is the way of life of a particular person or group of people. This includes the habits, attitudes, tastes, moral standards, economic level, etc., that together constitute the mode of living of an individual or group. When you make prayer a lifestyle it is normally recognized by others as a habit.

Prayer must be lived. As a believer, you should not go a day without praying. It must be YOU. When we talk about prayer being the believer's lifestyle, some questions need to come into play:

When do I pray?

Most of us have made prayer an occasional moment. We choose to pray based off of our feelings. We do not visit prayer when all is well with our lives, and will only resort to it when the storms of life come our way. Prayer is the defense mechanism of the believer. The more you pray the more you become a fortified city (person) because the daily prayers become not only a lifestyle but also a wall of protection for you. In answering the question of when we pray, I stand in agreement with the concept that *"praying always with all prayer and supplication in the Spirit, being watchful to this end with all perseverance and supplication for all the saints"* (**Ephesians 6:18**). The apostle Paul uses the word "**all**" four times in **Ephesians 6:18**. There's no pause button for the spiritual war. The devil doesn't sleep or take vacations. The spiritual war is always on—that's why we need to pray at all times.

Maybe you're tempted to think that it's actually impossible to pray at all times. You can't pray when you sleep! Is praying at all times even possible? Or maybe you think that since it's impossible to fulfill this command perfectly, we shouldn't even think about how to obey it.

Let's remember a couple of things. First, God isn't going to command something that is impossible. He will give us the ability to obey as He desires. Maybe we won't pray words to God every second of every day but maybe we'll live in a spirit of prayer that constantly talks with God and remembers His presence.

> **"**
> *In your bright days, pray,
> and in your dark moments,
> pray, because at all times
> God is ready to help you.*
> **"**

Secondly, instead of debating if it is possible to pray at all times or not, I think it is more productive to think of the opportunity that God gives us. Not everyone has access to God. But for those of us in Christ, "*we have boldness and access with confidence by faith.*" **(Ephesians 3:12)**

In your bright days, pray, and in your dark moments, pray, because at all times God is ready to help you. When the impossible sets in, pray. When you don't know if you can go on in the Christian life, pray. Even when all seems to be going well, pray, because we always need to be careful and never think we are standing firm. As Paul says in **1 Corinthians 10:12:** "*No* *temptation has overtaken you except such as is common to man; but God is faithful, who will not allow you to be tempted beyond what you are able, but with the temptation will also make the way of escape, that you may be able to bear it."*

Constant prayer that seeks the face of God deepens our communion with Him and the effectiveness of our prayers. *"If you abide in Me, and My words abide in you, you will ask what you desire, and it shall be done for you."* **(John 15:7)**

Brothers and sisters, this command to pray at all times should encourage us greatly.

Where do l pray?

Religion has led us to conclude that prayer must be done in the sanctuary. This has unfortunately become a norm for most believers who will only pray once they find themselves in the sanctuary. Surprisingly, prayer meetings have the smallest recorded attendance in the modern-day church. *"For where two or three are gathered together in My name, I am there in the midst of them."* **(Matthew 18:20)** The Holy Spirit dwells with us, and we can pray anywhere and at any time because He makes you two in order to fulfill scripture. As a believer, you have to build your own personal prayer altar where you can engage with and access your God.

Building a prayer altar is foundational in our pursuit of God's Presence. It is the starting place, the consistent place, the fueling place where we meet with God and create an environment for Him to come. This needs to happen personally, first. We then establish similar altars in our home as families and in our churches. It is from this place of personal encounter that we have the anointing and authority to counter the darkness in our communities and create a place for God to come and dwell.

Creating a sacred time and a sacred place takes practice and discipline. However, when you have decided that the call is worth the cost, you are in a position to receive the grace that will take you where you have never been—to a new place of encounter and relationship in the presence of the living God. As we learn to wait and linger in His presence we can expect to experience His tangible presence on a personal level, long before we ever experience it corporately. As we keep the fire burning in our own lives, we become the kindling for the corporate altars that must be established within our communities.

Prayer altars consist of reading God's Word, worshiping, listening, journaling, waiting, and "soaking" in His presence. It is where we practice quieting our hearts and tuning into the voice of the Holy Spirit. It is where we learn to "be", long before we "do." As our personal altars are established, we begin to experience the transformational power of His presence in our own lives which builds faith and expectation for corporate encounters of His presence.

Communities who have experienced a transforming revival have all established prayer altars as a precursor to a divine visitation. Though these prayer altars were usually established out of desperation and turmoil, the power of His supernatural presence is consistent. Even so, we do not have to wait until crisis hits. We can choose to establish prayer altars in our lives out of love and obedience. God has given us the choice to draw close to Him. We should respond to His invitation before we expect Him to respond to ours.

Jesus made prayer a lifestyle. He was always fulfilling the Word of God as indicated in **Job 38:1:** "*Have you commanded the morning since your days began, and caused the dawn to know its place*".

A man that has been marked by prayer might not appear as one of testimony in the eyes of man today, but so far as he has prayer deposited in him, he will surely manifest his destiny at all cost. A man of prayer is a man of power.

The hour of prayer and Bible reading are probably the most neglected disciplines of our spiritual walk. Jesus asked His disciples to tarry with him in prayer for one hour. Then He came to the disciples and found them sleeping, and said to Peter, *"What! Could you not watch with Me one hour?"* **(Matthew 26:40)** Are we willing to give Him one hour a day? God is calling for His church to awaken, to arise to righteousness (His way of doing and being right). This includes a life dedicated to prayer—communion with the Trinity and the great Three in One.

Prayer isn't something a person does; it is something he lives. Prayer is where you find mercy and grace. There are believers who desire to pray but don't know where to begin; others simply are void of the desire to pray.

What is your view of prayer? Do you allow time for developing a personal relationship with the God who purports the fulfillment of every person? Do you give Him a quick rundown of your prayer list and exit without giving Him time to build a fellowship with you? The Holy Spirit is your helper and He will help you develop your priorities in prayer.

5

THE PRAYING MAN

A prayerful man is a powerful man. Until you win the spiritual war, you cannot manifest physically. When you are prayerless, you are powerless and become vulnerable to the arrows and evil schemes from the camp of the enemy. It is about time the body of Christ brings to the attention of new converts that it is a good thing to accept Jesus as your Lord and Savior.

> *"If you confess that Jesus is Lord and believe that God raised him from death, you will be saved. For it is by our faith that we are put right with God; it is by our confession that we are saved."*
>
> — ROMANS 10:9-10

However, after confession you need to go through a class that will equip you and bring you to the understanding that you are God's treasure. That is when you have to pull yourself together for warfare.

"For we do not wrestle against flesh and blood, but against principalities, against powers, against the rulers of the darkness of this age, against spiritual hosts of wickedness in the heavenly places."

— EPHESIANS 6:12

Until you come to a full understanding of **Ephesians 6:12** you might not be able to activate the praying man in you. We need to renew our minds and come to an understanding that the spiritual realm controls the physical, and to be ready to engage in prayer at all times. The battle we are fighting is an unfair battle. We do not see our opponents but they have a clear vantage point into our lives.

The war involves powerful antagonists in extreme, desperate, hand-to-hand battle. Tremendous issues of life and death are at stake, for it is no ordinary combat. The word "against" stands out five times upon the page. We have an out-and-out adversary who is actively and aggressively warring against us, assisted by powerful and wicked allies.

"Not against flesh and blood." This statement clarifies the atmosphere immediately regarding the nature of our foe. The conflict is not with the human and the visible, but with the superhuman and the invisible. We do not belong to the same order of being or on the same plane of life as our foe.

Our enemy is not flesh and blood or people. Now I don't know about you, but this confuses me sometimes. I can see people, but I cannot see the unseen enemy. How quickly am I suckered into the trap of thinking that people are my enemy? I have said many times, "If it were not for people, I could live the Christian life." You've done it too. In your prayer time you may have said, "God, if You will just get rid of this person who is bothering me, it will be alright." We have this paranoia when it comes to people. We think people are our enemies. But it is that which controls the person that is my true enemy. That is why God consistently says in **Ephesians 4:3**, *"Be diligent to preserve the unity of the Spirit in the bonds of peace."* He is saying, "People, you are not each other's enemy." We mistakenly think people are our enemies: our boss, our husband, our wife, our children, people we work with, or whomever. We think if we can defeat them in some way, if we can get rid of them, we can have peace and victory. That is all upside down. We end up fighting each other. They are not our enemy. We use hateful words and provide unwanted criticism. We have to tear somebody else down to build ourselves up as if we are in some kind of competition with one another. We forget we are on the same team. Paul said, "Flesh and blood are not our enemy." If we fight we lose. The war was won at Calvary. We are not to be each other's enemy.

You may be saying now wait a minute! Flesh and blood are the ones bringing me all the harm. Flesh and blood are the ones injuring me. Do you understand? Paul is trying to say, "Hey, folks, you need to realize the war zone you are in is not with people. Our enemy is what controls the people."

When we begin to understand and discover the battlefield, God can give us His word of assurance. **II Corinthians 10:4-5:** *"For the weapons of our warfare are not carnal but mighty in God for pulling down strongholds, casting down arguments and every high thing that exalts itself against the knowledge of God, bringing every thought into captivity to the obedience of Christ."*

Let us consider the story in the Bible that pertains to the major prophet Elijah in **I Kings 18:20-46.**

From the account of the aforementioned story, I can conclude that Elijah was a praying man. This is the same man who had prayed for a drought over the land and had now come back to show himself to Ahab who was once after his life. I can boldly say that the years of his absence were nothing but preparation for destroying the enemy (the prophets of Baal). This remarkable drought lasted three-and-one-half years thanks to the fervent prayer of Elijah.

Earlier, God told Elijah to hide himself. Now it was time for him to present himself. There is a time to hide and to be alone with God, and there is also a time to present yourself to the world. Some wish to remain hidden when they should step up and present themselves. Elijah simply obeyed God's command. Though it happened through the prayers of Elijah, his prayers were sensitive to God's guidance. The drought did not begin or end as a result of Elijah's will, but by God's will. Elijah challenged King Ahab to gather the idol prophets of Baal and Asherah for this meeting at Mount Carmel. This was a God-inspired plan that Elijah obeyed. It was important to confront and eliminate these prophets of Baal before God sent rain to the land of Israel. It was crucial that everyone understand that the rain came from God, not from Baal.

It is hard to know why Ahab carried out the instructions of Elijah. Perhaps he hoped that the people would be so angry with Elijah for the last three years of drought that this crowd would turn against him and gather the prophets together on Mount Carmel: These prophets of Baal hated Elijah. They loved the favor of King

Ahab and Queen Jezebel and they enthusiastically promoted the persecution of any true follower of the Lord. But over the last three years, they had been severely humbled by Elijah and the drought that was sustained by his prayers. All their cries to the weather god Baal were ineffective. They hated this prophet of God who humiliated them and their sham priesthood so thoroughly. When you are a prayerful man, you are very sensitive and can indicate what the outcome of a moment is going to be. There were three things I came to discover when Elijah faced the prophets of Baal on Mount Carmel:

1. Elijah gave the prophets of Baal plenty of advantage. It was thought that Baal was the sky god, lord of the weather and the sender of lightning (thought to be fire from the sky). If Baal were real, he certainly could send fire from heaven.
2. He put God and himself on the line before the gathered nation of Israel, which took a lot of faith. Elijah learned this faith over many months of daily dependence on God, both at the Brook Cherith and at the widow's house at Zarapeth.
3. Elijah had plenty of reasons to have confidence in the LORD God. First, he was

following express instructions from the LORD. **(1 Kings 18:36)** Second, he knew from the history of Israel that God could and would send fire from heaven upon a sacrifice. **(Judges 6:20-21** and **2 Chronicles 7:1-7)**

The prophets of Baal had a devoted prayer life. They prayed for long hours and with great passion. Their worship was filled with enthusiasm and activity. Yet because they did not pray to the real God, their prayer meant nothing. The battle was no longer between Elijah and the prophets of Baal, but between Elohim and Baal—and who can stand against the King of Kings? When He shows up no one dares. He's the mighty God, who is great in battle; He has never lost any battle and will never come close to losing one. It was an already-won battle in the spirit and was only awaiting its physical manifestation.

I believe during the period of the droughts, the prophets of Baal did not engage their god to send down rain, and their attempt to do it now was going to be a struggle not only for them but their god as well. Elijah knew what God was up to and all he needed to do was to walk under the obedience of His voice in order to wipe out the prophets of Baal from the land and bring a new season to His people. The prophets of Baal had passion, commitment, sincerity, devotion, and great energy. They did not have a God in heaven who answered by fire. When the fire of God fell, its effect was beyond expectation. It would have been enough if merely the cut-up pieces of bull on the altar were ignited, but God wanted more than simple vindication. He wanted to glorify Himself among the people. At that moment, the people were completely persuaded. They were asked to choose between Baal and God. There was no choice to make, obviously, the LORD was God.

Elijah knew that once the official worship of Baal had been defeated, the purpose of the drought had been fulfilled. Rain was on the way. Elijah and Ahab would each now do what they wanted to do—Elijah would pray and Ahab would eat. After Elijah told Ahab to go up and eat, he went into prayer.

Most of us pray for the move of God's power and once we experience Him, we slow down or stop praying. But this wasn't the case with Elijah. His mission wasn't complete until he came back and showed himself to Ahab. He wasn't going to hold off with prayer. He bowed down on the ground and put his face between his knees. This was an unusual posture of prayer for Elijah. He wasn't kneeling, sitting, standing, or lying prostrate before the LORD. This shows that the power in prayer resides in faith in the living God. This was also a persistent prayer. It was as if Elijah would not take "no" for an answer, because he had confidence that God's will was to send rain.

As believers, let us not be dejected by disappointment, but continue to wait upon God, who will answer us. God's promises are only given through prayer and they show the direction in which we may ask, and the extent to which we may expect an answer. Elijah prayed, asking in faith for God to send the rain. Elijah obviously sensed this was the will of God, yet it was his fervent prayer that brought the rain. The evidence of the rain came slowly and in a small way, but out of this small evidence God brought a mighty work. There was a word of faith from Elijah to Ahab. Based only on the sighting of a cloud that was as small as a man's hand, he knew a heavy downpour of rain was on the way.

The sky became black with clouds and wind. So Ahab rode away and went to Jezreel. Then the hand of the LORD came upon Elijah and he girded his loins and ran ahead of Ahab to the entrance of Jezreel. There was a heavy rain; God's word through Elijah was proven true. The long drought was over and it was demonstrated that the prayers of Elijah both withheld the rain and then subsequently brought the rain. The overtaken anointing was also demonstrated here.

I beseech you not to just be a believer, but a believer who is prayerful and also obedient to the voice of God and walks as His Spirit directs you. Let us not forget, *"And from the days of John the Baptist until now the kingdom of heaven suffers violence, and the violent take it by force."* **(Matthew 11:12)**

6

PRAY WITHOUT CEASING

G rowing up as a child in Africa, I came to the realization that this particular church in my neighborhood was always having prayer sessions from Monday to Friday. All I said then was, "Why do these people worry God?"

The members of the church would always give the same answer: "We come to wait on God."

Interestingly, I didn't always see the same people coming in to wait, and that made me draw the conclusion that once they received an answer, they'd go on holiday, just as most of us do.

As believers, it is good to come before the altar of God in the church to pray as Hannah did: "*Then she made a vow and said, 'O Lord of hosts, if You will indeed look on the affliction of Your maidservant and remember me, and not forget Your maidservant, but will give Your maidservant a male child, then I will give him to the Lord all the days of his life, and no razor shall come upon his head.*'" (**1 Samuel 1:1**)

But we also need to have our own prayer altar at home where we can encounter God at all times.

The life of Jesus was all about prayer. Right from the beginning of His ministry, till the time He was on the cross, He laid a foundation of prayer by fasting and praying for forty days and forty nights. Before He was baptized by John, He was in a prayer mood, which was proven when the disciples came up to him and said "Teach us how to pray." All they saw Jesus do was pray.

Understand that praying without ceasing means that our prayers as Christians should be unlimited. We should not set a specific time for ourselves when it comes to prayer, rather we must live prayer. The moment you wake up in the morning should not be a time for social media as our generation has come to believe. It should be a solemn moment of facing God in prayer. If I were asked "What time should a person pray?" my answer would simply be, pray at all times. In every activity that you find yourself, involve prayer.

Often, we come to a place of prayer when we are going through the storms of life. Until we make prayer a practice, we will not be able to be devoted to it. Every great man who ever lived in the Bible prayed and the result is that we are now getting to know about them.

When the Bible says pray without ceasing, that does not mean that saints should be always on their knees, ever lifting up their hands, and vocally calling upon God. But believers should be found daily in the performance of this duty.

The Bible often says pray frequently. Do not put off praying, or cease from prayer because of the prevalence of sin, the temptations of Satan, or through general discouragement because an answer is not immediately received, or through human negligence; but be consistent in prayer and pray often. The widow in **Luke 18:1-8** did not give up, but instead was consistently at the door of the judge. Widows in the ancient world were incredibly vulnerable, regularly listed with orphans and aliens as those persons deserving of special protection. The fact that this particular widow had to beseech a judge unattended by any family highlights her extreme vulnerability. Yet she not only asked the judge fervently, but also persisted in her pleas for justice to the point of creating sufficient pressure to influence the judge's actions. This is synonymous with the process of prayer between humans and God. Without vulnerability and persistence the Lord cannot intervene on our behalf. This is why we should not just pray in times of trouble and distress, but must be consistent in our communication with God.

It appears that during our communication with God, we as humans are no longer praying but complaining, and that is gradually pushing us away from God. However, **James 5:13-16** highlights that prayer should not just be used because you are at your lowest point, but should be performed at any given time during your life, whether things are good or bad.

> *"Is anyone among you suffering? Let him pray. Is anyone cheerful? Let him sing psalms. Is anyone among you sick? Let him call for the elders of the church, and let them pray over him, anointing him with oil in the name of the Lord. And the prayer of faith will save the sick, and the Lord will raise him up. And if he has committed sins, he will be forgiven. Confess your trespasses to one another, and pray for one another, that you may be healed. The effective, fervent prayer of a righteous man avails much."*

— Vs.13-16

In conclusion, I will outline four ways that help us to pray without ceasing:

1.) Begin with gratitude

> *"Enter his gates with thanksgiving and his courts with praise; give thanks to him and praise his name."*

— Psalm 100:4

In other words, start by telling God what you're thankful for. Prayer doesn't have to be asking for something; it can simply be thanking Him from your heart for what He has already done.

2.) Get real

In **Luke 18:9-14**, a Pharisee, obsessed by his own virtue, is contrasted with a tax collector who humbly asks God for mercy. Prayer is simply a conversation. Talk to Him the way you would talk to a friend. Sit down and just let the words pour out, casually, simply. Just be real.

3.) Sing a song of praise

> *"Is anyone among you in trouble? Let them pray. Is anyone happy? Let them sing songs of praise."*
>
> — JAMES 5:13

Often, we think of prayer as what to do when we need God to fix something or when we're unhappy. But the Bible encourages us to pray at all times. Remember the idea of prayer being like a radio playing in the background all the time? Make that literal by listening to worship music. As you sing along, offer it to God as your prayer. Or make up your own song along the way.

Nobody is listening but Him, so don't worry if you're out of tune.

4.) Give up worrying

> *"Do not be anxious about anything, but in every situation, by prayer and petition, with thanksgiving, present your requests to God."*

> — PHILIPPIANS 4:6

We are not meant to worry. We also waste too many minutes doing just that. Next time something weighs heavy on your heart, envision yourself extending it up to God and letting Him hold it for you. Ask Him what your role is and if there is something you need to do, do it. Do not take back the weight of the worry. Start thanking God for who He is and what He has already done for you, and you will feel the weight lifting off your shoulders as the words come.

7

PRAYER MY WEAPON

Life is filled with mystery and until we begin to dig deeper into the twist and turns of this life, and begin to discover and understand the things that fight against us, we may not make it to the top as God has destined us to. The modern-day Christian will pray their way to the top but may end up not maintaining the higher heights with prayer. We live in a privileged place where we have to be mindful of who we are and then understand the battles that comes with it. *"And from the days of John the Baptist until now the kingdom of heaven suffers violence, and the violent take it by force."* **(Matthew 11:12)** Understand that the one you are wrestling with is not gentle but violent; very disciplined when it comes to carrying out wickedness and unwilling to let go until they are successful.

"For they sleep not, except they have done mischief; and their sleep is taken away, unless they cause some to fall. For they eat the bread of wickedness, and drink the wine of violence."

— PROVERBS 4:16-17

As a believer, you need a weapon that you can use against the enemy on the battlefield and it's none other than prayer. Prayer is the believer's weapon and we have to activate it at all times. We become vulnerable when we lose our prayer guard. We are soldiers of our Lord's army and must be ready for battle at all times. *"For we do not wrestle against flesh and blood, but against principalities, against powers, against the rulers of the darkness of this age, against spiritual hosts of wickedness in the heavenly places."* **(Ephesians 6:12)** It is not a physical battle but a spiritual one, and the only weapon we can use in this war is prayer.

In this chapter, I am going to talk about an encounter in the Bible that demonstrates prayer as a weapon. Let us look into the story of Paul and Silas according to **Acts 16:16-32.**

Paul and Silas were missionaries who traveled from place to place to spread the gospel of our Lord and savior Jesus Christ. Their missionary work took them to Philippi where they meet a businesswoman named

Lydia, a cloth dealer. She and her whole household had been baptized after learning about Jesus. Lydia urged the missionaries to stay at her home—she was a woman of some wealth and could provide for everyone —and they agreed. Paul and Silas stayed and used her house as a home base, and each day they headed out to preach and share the gospel with others. As they were doing this each day, they encountered a slave girl who brought her owners a lot of money by telling people's fortunes, for she had a "spirit of divination." When she saw Paul and the others, she started to follow them and yell out, "These men are servants of the Most High God, who proclaim to you a way of salvation." She did this every day.

The lifestyle of this damsel is even found in our day and time. There are a lot of people out there who can call on the name of Jesus, make you believe they know Him and hide behind His name with hidden agendas.

"Not everyone who says to Me, 'Lord, Lord,' shall enter the kingdom of heaven, but he who does the will of My Father in heaven. Many will say to Me in that day, 'Lord, Lord, have we not prophesied in Your name, cast out demons in Your name, and done many wonders in Your name?' And then I will declare to them, 'I never knew you; depart from Me, you who practice lawlessness!'"

— LUKE 6:21-23

Like many who have what the scriptures call an "unclean spirit" or are in some way "possessed by spirits," the slave girl was not saying anything that was untrue. But her following Paul and Silas around didn't help them find the nice introduction to talking about Jesus that they had hoped for.

"Beware of false prophets, who come to you in sheep's clothing, but inwardly they are ravenous wolves. You will know them by their fruits. Do men gather grapes from thorn bushes or figs from thistles? Even so, every good tree bears good fruit, but a bad tree bears bad fruit. A good tree cannot bear bad fruit, nor can a bad tree bear good fruit. Every tree that does not bear good fruit is cut down and thrown into the fire. Therefore by their fruits you will know them."

— MATTHEW 7:15-20

According to the Book of Acts, Paul was "very much annoyed." And so, prompted apparently by his annoyance rather than a desire to heal the girl, Paul ordered the spirit to come out of her in the name of Jesus Christ. And it did. There is power in association, and Paul noticed that if he did not rebuke the spirit that was operating within the girl, it would affect their missionary work.

Most of us in our life journey have entertained people who carry negative energy and make us drift from our purpose and destiny. But suddenly this slave girl had lost her money-making capacity for her owners. It did not sit well with them. Her owners seized Paul and Silas, dragged them to the local magistrates, and claimed: *"These men are disturbing our city; they are*

Jews [they did not know they were Romans] *and are advocating customs that are not lawful for us as Romans to adopt or observe."* (Acts 16:20-21) The crowds joined in with the accusations, and the local authorities had them stripped, beaten and flogged, and thrown in prison. The prison guard put them in the innermost cell and fastened their feet in the stocks.

Prisons in Biblical times were not nice places at all. "Prison time" was not a typical sentence—prison was merely a holding place for those awaiting trial, and sometimes release, but often another punishment or execution. Prisons were overcrowded, and the inner cells, which Acts is careful to note was where Paul and Silas were held, would have been entirely dark. The iron chains used to bind prisoners were heavy, and particularly painful to bodies that had just been beaten and flogged. Hygiene was lacking. Food was minimal and most prisoners had to rely on visitors to sustain them with food and drink of any substance. Many prisoners would be kept together in one cell. It was a dreadful situation. They never questioned God and never complained, but reminded themselves that the battle is beyond the physical and that all they could do was activate and engage their prayer weapon.

Somehow, Paul and Silas found the strength to spend their time in prison praying and singing hymns. It was midnight, and the scripture makes us understand that other prisoners heard and were listening to them. Imagine them all in the stifling darkness, with Paul and Silas lifting them up with words of hope. Suddenly, there was an earthquake. The quaking caused the doors of the prison to open, and the chains of all the prisoners to fall off. Not only did they activate their weapon of prayer, they also invoked the presence of God through the singing of hymns. Their worship left God with no choice but to come and dwell with them. Whenever you worship God during your life struggles, He becomes a warship and will fight all of your battles on your behalf.

The jailer woke, saw the chaos, and got ready to take his own life, despairing at his complete failure. But Paul and Silas had not escaped and nor had any other prisoners, for whatever reason. Paul spoke to prevent the jailer from hurting himself, and the jailer rushed in with a light, fell down before Paul and Silas, and asked what he must do to be saved. Apparently, he knew enough about what Paul and Silas had been arrested for to know they had some compelling message to share.

Paul and Silas told the jailer about Jesus. They shared the good news of God's grace not just with him, but with the whole household. And the jailer and his family decided to be baptized and to become Jesus- followers without delay. They fed Paul and Silas, and cared for their wounds, and kept them in the house instead of the prison.

In conclusion, prayer is a weapon. The physical is controlled by the spiritual. The moment you lift up your prayer to God, you engage the spiritual because the words you speak, as they go to the Father, are translated into a spiritual language, and He interprets them to your favor. Keep activating your weapon of prayer, it always works for us and makes us victorious in our daily life battles.

8

BENEFITS OF PRAYER

P rayer is work, and if you are not disciplined, devoted, and dedicated to it, you will fall out along the way. This work I am referring to, as with all other jobs, comes with benefits. There are a lot of benefits we derive from prayer, but in this chapter I will pay attention to four of them.

1.) Prayer increases our faith in God

Because prayer is our communion with God, each time we approach the Lord through prayer, our faith strengthens. God promises that He hears the prayers of His people.

> *"Now this is the confidence that we have in Him, that if we ask anything according to His will, He hears us."*

> — 1 JOHN 5:14

As we see God answer our prayers, with both positive and negative responses, our faith matures because we realize He is actively present in our lives.

Hannah's prayer life in **1 Samuel 1:2**: *"And Hannah prayed and said: My heart rejoices in the Lord; My horn is exalted in the Lord. I smile at my enemies, Because I rejoice in Your salvation. No one is holy like the Lord, For there is none besides You, Nor is there any rock like our God."* This Bible verse illustrates personal growth through prayer. All she said in this prayer is, this is the faith I have in you, so glorify your name in my life. (Supporting scriptures: **Hebrews 11:6, Proverbs 3:5-6**)

2.) Prayer deepens fellowship with God

Through prayer, we learn the heart of our Heavenly Father. King David, known as a man after God's own heart—*"But now thy kingdom shall not continue: The Lord hath sought him a man after his own heart, and the Lord hath commanded him to be captain over his people, because thou hast not kept that which the Lord commanded thee"* (**1 Samuel 13:14**)—recorded many of his prayers to God in the Book of Psalms. Through not only our own expression of faith, but also in times of stillness, we are able to deepen the depth of our relationship with the Lord. We should not be in a rush to leave the presence of God when we pray but rather wait to hear Him speak back to us. (Supporting scriptures: **Jeremiah 33:1-3, 1 Corinthians 2:9-13**)

3.) Prayer helps us discern and accept God's will

When Jesus' disciples asked Him how to pray, one part of his prayer was to ask that God's will be done on earth as it is in heaven. **(Matthew 6:10)** Through this petition, we learn the importance of discerning and accepting God's will for our lives. By communing with God, we avail ourselves to submit to His authority. After Jesus wrestled in prayer at Gethsemane, he was ready to suffer the cross because he knew it was his to bear. For us, when we seek the Lord, peace comes at the knowledge of His will. (Supporting scriptures: **Lamentations 3:25, Philippians 1:9, Colossians 1:9**)

4.) Prayer makes us powerful

When men pray, powerful things happen. Objects in the universe shift in your favor. A praying man is a powerful man. When Joshua prayed, *"so the sun stood still, and the moon stopped, till the people had revenge upon their enemies."* **(Joshua 10:1)** The moment you open up your mouth to pray and do not doubt, you receive God's backing. At this point, the words you speak are no longer your words but of the One who lives inside of you. *"You are of God, little children, and have overcome* *them, because He who is in you is greater than he who is in the world."* (1 John 4:4) (Supporting scriptures **Joshua 10, Jeremiah 51:20-23**)

I urge you to increase your prayer life, for the best awaits you.

_____

9

TWENTY-ONE PRAYER POINTS

This chapter is comprised of categories of prayer points to help us with our daily prayers:

THANKSGIVING

1.) Pray and thank the Lord for the gift of life He's bestowed on you. One of the greatest gifts is to be alive, and for that you have to be thankful to God. This prayer covers you, your family and loved ones. **(Psalm 124)**

2.) Command your being to thank the Lord for everything He has made you, both outward and inward. Even if you are not feeling well in any part of your body, command it to be thankful. You will be amazed the healing power that can bring you. **(Psalm 150:6, Psalm 103)**

3.) Pray and thank the Lord for the life of your leaders and those in authority. This includes your pastor and his family, those who represent your districts, county, state and the president and his family. **(1 Timothy 2:2, Proverbs 21:1-3)**

FORGIVENESS

4.) Pray and ask God to touch the heart of whoever you have wronged in any way, knowingly or unknowingly, and give unto them the spirit of forgiveness to let go. Pray and forgive whoever has wronged you in any way. Let go and let God. Most people have lost their breakthrough because of unforgiving hearts. **(Matthew 6:12, Ephesians 4:31-32, 1 John 1:9, 2 Chronicles 7:14, Romans 5:8)**

PROTECTION

5.) Pray that the Lord will be unto you a pillar of cloud during the day and a pillar of fire at night. God had to be a pillar of cloud for the Israelites as they journeyed unto the promised land because they had not been trained for battle. He had to hide them from any group of people who might see them coming and try to attack them. He prevented poisonous and deadly animals from attacking them, and also provided for them light and warmth at night. **(Exodus 13:21-22, Exodus 14:19-20)**

6.) Pray that the Lord will increase His protection over your life from the crown of your head to the soles of your feet and put the devourer to shame for your sake. In reading the scriptures connected to this prayer points, replace your name with the words "I" and "YOU". **(Psalm 91)**

7.) Pray that the Lord will rise on your behalf and fight anyone who rises against you so that the glory of the Lord will be made manifest in your life. **(Psalm 3)**

8.) Pray that the Lord will encamp His angels in charge of warfare around you and fight against those who seek your life. **(2 Kings 6:15-19, Psalm 35)**

DELIVERANCE

9.) Pray that the Lord deliver you from all evil. **(Matthew 6:13)**

10.) Pray that the Lord keep His angels over you and order your steps. **(Psalm 91:11-12)**

11.) Pray that the Lord deliver you from bloodthirsty men. **(Psalm 59:2)**

12.) Pray that the Lord deliver you from all of your fears. "Fear not" is repeated 365 times in the Bible, so in God's infinite wisdom He wants us to take a daily dose of FEAR NOT, thus completing the yearly prescription.

OPEN DOORS

13.) Pray and command every gate and everlasting door that stands in the way of breakthrough to open so that the King of Glory will enter and you will follow. This prayer can be prayed when you are going for interviews, or entering a country, state or a community for the first time. **(Psalm 24:7-10, Isaiah 45:1)**

14.) Pray that your gates of miracles, testimonies and breakthroughs will be continually opened. **(Isaiah 60:11, Isaiah 22:22)**

DESTINY HELPERS

15.) Pray and ask God to place your matters on the minds of your destiny helpers and connect you to them. **(Esther 6:1-3)**

16.) Pray and call forth your destiny helpers from the north, south, east and west to locate you and ask God to open your eyes to see them when they come your way. **(Genesis 18:2-3, 1 Samuel 10:3-7)**

DOMINION

17.) Pray that you will experience dominion from now in Jesus' name. **(Genesis 1:26-28, Matthew 16:19)**

18.) Pray that the Lord will enlarge you and extend your coast. **(1 Chronicles 4:10)**

FAVOR

19.) Pray that the favor of the Lord will locate you and your household. **(Esther 2:15-17, Luke 1:28)**

LONGEVITY

20.) Pray and decree over your life that you will live to fulfill the number of your days. This must be a daily prayer. **(Psalm 118:17, 3 John 1:2)**

PURPOSE

21.) Pray that the Lord grant you the grace to fulfill your purpose in the land of the living. **(Philippians 3:14-15, John 5:30, Psalm 143:10)**

CONCLUSION

In view of all we have discussed, understand that prayer, being a form of communication, needs a dialogue. Once you speak to Elohim, you need to wait for Him to speak back to you. Let us be addicted to prayer, for it's a weapon for a believer. There is no holiday when it comes to praying.

" *Let prayer be YOU* "

Don't wait for the storms of life to come your way before you make time to pray, but let it be a practice. Let prayer be YOU.

The commodity of the heavenly bank is prayer.

Therefore, one should invest daily in prayer to receive the returns and benefits. A prayerful man is a powerful man.

" *A prayerful man is a powerful man* "

ABOUT THE AUTHOR

Stephen Morgan Asamoa Boakye

There is nothing greater than having peace of mind, in knowing that God aligns people within their purpose to serve others with a selfless and grateful heart. Stephen accepted his call into ministry five years ago and currently serves under the able leadership of Dr. Sonnie Badu at The Rockhill Church as a Pastor. Stephen has been an active member and integral part of The Rockhill Church since its establishment, gracefully reflecting God's divine goodness as he serves.

Born in Winneba, Central Region of Ghana, Stephen accepts and believes his purpose of fulfilling the will of God for his life as well as for the people around him. He acknowledges the times and dispensation that the name of the Lord must be magnified. He is compelled to go out and impact lives through spreading the word of God that those who have fallen into the lassitude of despair might arise to possess the City Gates.

In order to fulfill God's purpose and to pursue his vision, Stephen committed himself to higher education by attending Trinity University of Ambassadors on scholarship from the school and The Rockhill Church where he obtained his Bachelor's degree in Christian Ministry. These classes have given him the opportunity to broaden his understanding of the content and contexts of the Bible. That exposure and other divine revelations birthed his first ever book, *The Praying Bank*.

The inspiration for this book is based on the understanding that prayer is not wasted and there is no such thing as "taking a break" when it comes to prayer. He believes that just as we try to save money in the bank we also need to invest prayer into our spiritual bank so in times of trouble we are able to make a withdrawal. This he believes is one of his most heartfelt and rewarding achievements.

NOTES

1. What Is Prayer?

1. "Prayer" (2021); *Wikipedia;* Retrieved from https://en.wikipedia. org/wiki/Prayer (Accessed 2 March 2021)

2. The Prayer Model

1. Anonymous (2019); "Forgiveness: Your Health Depends On It." *Johns Hopkins Medicine.* Retrieved from https://www.hopkinsmedicine. org/health/wellness-and-prevention/forgiveness-your-health-depends-on-it (Accessed 2 March 2021)
2. Hostetler, B; *How to Pray;* Feb 19 2016

3. Types of Prayer

1. Badu, S (2019) *Dynamics Of Prayer*; Available at https://www. youtube.com/watch?v=DcMoeoXQBzw (Accessed 2 March 2021)
2. Badu, S (2019) *The Power of Prayer;* Available at https://www. youtube.com/watch?v=DcMoeoXQBzw (Accessed 2 March 2021)
3. Badu, S (2019) *Seven Benefits of Prayer;* Available at https://www. youtube.com/watch?v=DcMoeoXQBzw (Accessed 2 March 2021)